Discussion Guide
and Exercises

for

What Does It Mean
To Be A Manager?

Five Phases of Employee Performance
and Eighteen Tasks of Management

Gil Herman

For information about this title, or to order other materials, contact the author:
Gil Herman
Managing Horizons
Gil@ManagingHorizons.com
708-207-1879

PREFACE

Many companies are using <u>What Does It Mean To Be A Manager?</u> for management skills training and review. I was asked to provide a discussion guide or workbook to optimize the conversations. Many readers will possibly feel this is not needed, and that's terrific. Go for it in whatever ways work for you. I'd love to hear your success stories. For others, this may serve as an enhancement for deepening your learning. I would also greatly value your feedback and would be happy to offer whatever assistance I can.

Gil Herman
<u>Gil@ManagingHorizons.com</u>

Table of Contents

Who is this guide for?   1
Some possible ways to use the guide   2
Chapter 1: Employee Performance Phases   4
Chapter 2: FORMULATE and ARTICULATE   6
Chapter 3: DESIGNATE   8
Chapter 4: INITIATE   10
Chapter 5: COMMUNICATE   12
Chapter 6: ENCULTURATE   14
Chapter 7: MOTIVATE   16
Chapter 8: EDUCATE   18
Chapter 9: PARTICIPATE   20
Chapter 10: PARTICIPATE - Part 2   22
Chapter 11: PARTICIPATE - Part 3   24
Chapter 12: EVALUATE   26
Chapter 13: PARTICIPATE - Part 4   28
Chapter 14: DELEGATE   30
Chapter 15: DELEGATE - Part 2   32
Chapter 16: DELEGATE - Part 3   34
Chapter 17: ELEVATE   36
Chapter 18: ELIMINATE, REMEDIATE
            and REINTEGRATE   38
Chapter 19: MIGRATE   40
Chapter 20: TERMINATE   42
Chapter 21: RUMINATE   44

Who is this guide for?

The book, <u>What Does It Mean To Be A Manager? Five Phases of Employee Performance and Eighteen Tasks of Management</u> and this guide have multiple audiences. In no particular order, it is designed for:

    1. Someone new to management seeking to learn proven best practices to expedite their learning curve

    2. An experienced manager seeking to review proven best practices to validate their own practice and perhaps pick up a few new ideas

    3. A manager of managers seeking to coach his/her management team around general management practices or specific opportunities for improvement

    4. HR personnel seeking a resource to assist in general management development or to coach an individual manager around a particular set of management tasks

    5. People wondering what it means to be a manager – either because they want to better understand their boss and/or because they aspire to be a manager someday

Some possible ways to use the guide

This guide provides some chapter-by-chapter discussion possibilities and/or exercises you may want to use. I've used past tense in the questions, assuming some experience. If this is your first time through any of the tasks, respond with how you plan to approach the task.

1. As an individual, read the chapters in sequence or based on your own interests and challenges. Take your own notes; make your own binder. Imagine you're Ariel as "we" talk. What other experiences would you share? What other questions do you have? Do some of the exercises that Ariel did.

2. With one or more of your peers, read the chapters one at a time or in clusters. Share your own experiences with each other. Reflect on your positive management experiences and create your own list of best practices. Reflect on experiences that – in hindsight – you wish had gone differently. If you could live through it again, what might you do to possibly bring about a better outcome? With your peers, add to the list of best practices the learnings from your "mistakes".

3. With your manager, have a series of one-to-one conversations about what you are reading in the book. Solicit feedback on how you show up in the various management tasks – what you do well and opportunities for being even better. Offer similar feedback to your manager as to how you experience his/her management behavior.

4. Perhaps you are interviewing candidates for management positions in your organization. With a little modification, some of the discussion questions may be useful in a behavioral interview.

5. Perhaps you are interviewing for a managerial position. Use the questions to prepare for your interview. Many of the questions ask about an organization's philosophies or practices. Asking those questions of your potential employer may help you determine fit.

Chapter 1: Employee Performance Phases

1.How does your experience (or that of others you've observed) "validate" the five-phase model?

2. Was it always clear to you which phase you were in – or at least when you were making a transition? Why do you think it was clear or unclear for you?

3. When you started in your current position, were you clear about the Target Performance Level? What difference did that make? What does it suggest about what was done in the Framing phase?

4. How have you experienced the upward slope of the Sustaining phase over time?

5. Assuming you currently have – or at least aspire to have – some supervisory responsibilities, how did you demonstrate that you were ready for a promotion? What feedback did you get about that potential and timing?

6. Have you ever experienced draining in your own performance? If so, what was that like for you? How did you get back on track?

7. What have you observed of someone in the Draining phase (other than any of your direct reports)? What did you learn from observing how other managers or employees handled the situation?

Exercise:

Make a timeline of your work history. You may want to include volunteer work or internship positions as well. Approach this in a series of steps, each providing deeper clarity.

1. Map out the overall timeline of when you began and when you transitioned from each organization.

2. Within each time period, further break out your timeline by position and for how long you were Training, Sustaining, Gaining, and/or Draining.

3. Think back over each segment of your timeline. What trends do you notice in your work history? How would you tell your story of going through the phases? Here are some possibilities:

* You were often a quick study and got up to the Target Performance Level in a short time.

* Once you were in the Sustaining phase, you were comfortable and confident that you could do all that was required of you.

* Typically you are chomping at the bit, ready to take on more and more responsibility.

* You always left a position because you were not feeling challenged.

Chapter 2: FORMULATE and ARTICULATE

1. What are the vision, mission, values and strategies of your organization? What is your organization's answer to "Why do we exist?"

2. What are the SMART goals for your team/department/division/company?

3. How do you ensure your SMART goals are in alignment with the rest of the organization? What do you do if they are not? How important is it for you to know the SMART goals of other managers and why?

4. Inevitably some goals change during a performance cycle. In your experience, what kinds of things lead to those changes? How effectively have the changes been communicated?

5. Which, if any, of your current goals seem to have shifted? Why? Are you and your manager in sync about those changes? To what extent are your various other stakeholders aware of your goals and priorities?

6. Consider each of your direct reports. Have any of their goals shifted since they were first articulated and committed to? Why? Are you and those direct reports in sync about those changes? How do you know?

Exercises:

1. List the strategic goals for the entire organization. Make a diagram to show how each of your team/department's SMART goals is directly connected to one or more of the goals of the entire organization. This should clarify how your team/department contributes to the results of the overall organization.
2. Do you have any team/department goals for which you cannot see a direct connection? Either clarify how they might be connected, or question why you have those goals.
3. Complete a similar exercise for each of your employee's goals. Be sure to discuss the connections with your employees so they understand the importance and relevance of what they are being asked to do.

Chapter 3: DESIGNATE

1. Describe a time you had an open position to fill on your staff. How was it determined that there was a position to fill? Who owned the decision about who would be hired?

2. Did you ever have one or more internal candidates to consider? How did you work through the selection process with them?

3. What have been some of your best practices for sourcing internal/external candidates?

4. Describe how effective the position requirements were with respect to "must have" and "nice-to-have" qualifications. Were you clear (and in agreement with others) as to the relative importance of each qualification?

5. Describe your interviewing process, including such things as who asks what questions, how many interviews are conducted, how you track the responses, and how you compare and select the candidates. Do you do it the same way every time? If not, what reasons do you have for what's different?

6. Who, when, and how do you share what about your organization with a candidate?

7. In what ways has HR been involved in the DESIGNATE task? What are some best practices? What could possibly be improved?

8. If and how did you test skills and knowledge? If and how did you assess cultural fit?

9. How was compensation determined? When was the offer made? Who can negotiate what?

10. As you think about your current process what is necessary, relevant, and sufficient? What could be changed to be even better?

Exercise:

Consider a position on your team that is currently not staffed. If you don't have an open position, either choose one that is filled or "dream up" a new position that could add further value to your team. Go through the process outlined in the book including:

* define the need for the position
* create/edit a job description, determining must-have and nice-to-have skills, knowledge, and culture fit
* write questions that could/will be used for interviews
* create a tracking sheet
* and so on

You might want to review your work with your manager and/or HR.

Chapter 4: INITIATE

1. What's been your best experience of being on-boarded at any organization or position? What were some of the reasons it was a good experience?

2. What's been a poor experience for you in on-boarding with an organization or position? What were some of the reasons it didn't work for you? What would you recommend as possible process changes for that organization?

3. In your organization, what paperwork has to be completed by a new employee? How much time do they have to complete it? What ideas do you have on how to make that task more efficient?

4. When you've made new hires – or perhaps transitioned current employees onto your team from elsewhere in the organization – how have you helped them understand their roles and goals?

5. Look over the 12 P's of INITIATE: Position, Projects, Process, People, Partner(s), Place, Provisions, Paperwork, Power, Publicity, Past/Present/Potential, and Probation. Which do you/your organization do well? Where is there opportunity for improvement? Do you have another category (especially if it starts with a "P") to add to this list?

Exercises:

1. Review your organization's on-boarding practices. Talk with your manager, peers, and direct reports to gather ideas for what works well and what doesn't.
2. If you feel there are some missing parts to your on-boarding practices, design ways to incorporate other practices into your process. Share your ideas with others – especially HR – so others can adopt or enhance your recommendations.

Chapter 5: COMMUNICATE

1. Describe a time when you had assumptions about a situation and checked them out before taking action. How did that help you get to a better decision?

2. Describe a time when you and another person "missed each other" in your communication. Using the Ladder of Inference, can you now identify where the conversation may have gone awry? If you could rewind the conversation, what would you do differently?

3. Do you agree that sometimes slowing down your conversation can lead to better decisions? Explain.

4. Describe a "whiplash conversation" you have had. What did you do – or could you have done – to help set context?

5. What are examples of clues you've picked up from someone's body language? How did you utilize those clues to improve the conversation?

6. In your conversations with your employees, what percent of the time are you talking versus listening? Of the time you're talking, what's the mix between making statements versus asking questions? How is your current style working for you?

7. Describe a time you've had a "meta-conversation". What led to having that discussion? What changed as a result?

8. Refer to the Thomas-Killmann conflict modes. Which mode(s) do you tend to operate in? How does that vary depending on the person or situation? Is your process intentional or a default setting?

Exercises:

1. Practice using the Ladder of Inference to slow down an important conversation in order to make a better decision. You might alert the other person that you're practicing this and why; then invite that person to work along with you.
2. Consider a person – business or personal – with whom you feel the need for a "meta-conversation" to improve the communication and the relationship. Invite that person to engage with you about whatever it is.
3. Consider how you tend to manage differences with someone important to you. Practice getting toward win-win solutions by clarifying and confirming what's important to each of you and why.

Chapter 6: ENCULTURATE

1. How do you describe the culture of your organization? How does it seem that people in your organization are aware of cultural norms?

2. Is the culture in your part of the organization the same as the rest of the organization – or is there something unique? Why is that?

3. How do you talk about culture with your employees? What difference does it make to have those conversations?

4. What rituals or taboos seem to be a part of your culture? Consider such things as work environment, dress codes, work hours and breaks, work ethic, who talks to whom about what, how decisions are made, etc.

5. What are the espoused values of your organization? How well do individual behaviors align with those values?

Exercises:

1. Imagine you are an anthropologist observing your organization at work. Describe what you see as if you were explaining how things work to someone who doesn't work at your organization.

2. Choose a value espoused by your organization. Talk with your manager, peers, and employees to explore what that value means and how it could show up more in everyone's behaviors. You might want to follow a process similar to Ariel's exploration about the meaning of "trust".

Chapter 7: MOTIVATE

1. Typically, how have you thought of what it means to motivate someone? Did anything change as you read this chapter?

2. How do you measure your success? What is it you want to do, have, and be? For you, how much is enough?

3. How do you describe how your path and the organization's path are sharing a journey? How has that evolved during your time with the organization?

4. What are your thoughts about the Motivation Hierarchy? Does this model resonate with you? What experiences/feelings do you have that align with the model? What differs?

5. How has your motivation changed over time? What have you done to increase your motivation/level of engagement, especially if it was starting to wane?

Exercises:

1. Engage in a conversation with one of your direct reports about what is important to him/her and why. You may want to use the 5-Whys process to help him/her explore what's really important. Your intent is to help clarify where he/she is on the Motivation Hierarchy and for you to understand even better how to align your work requests with the level of motivation.
2. Engage in a conversation with one of your direct reports to explore how his/her path intersects with the organization's path and what you are asking that person to do. Perhaps use this question: "What's important to you in your life that working here helps you do, have, or be?"

Chapter 8: EDUCATE

1. How have your managers helped you get to the Target Performance Level in various positions?

2. What have you done in the Training phase to help an employee develop the skills and knowledge needed to move to the Sustaining phase?

3. Consider the three parts of positive performance feedback. Which part do you consider the easiest to identify? Which part do you consider is most powerful for the recipient? Explain.

4. What are some good examples of corrective feedback that you have provided? What makes you say they were good?

5. What have been some of the more challenging aspects of providing corrective feedback to someone? Imagine you could rewind the clock and do it again. What would you change and why?

6. How have you known and acknowledged that someone is transitioning to the Sustaining phase?

Exercises:

1. Identify a recent positive outcome achieved by one of your direct reports. Prepare and deliver a positive reinforcement feedback utilizing the three parts described in the book.

2. Identify a recent behavior or result by one of your direct reports that did not produce what you expected or wanted. Determine what level of corrective feedback might be appropriate. Sometimes simply restating the request and the reason why will be sufficient to change the behavior. Other times, there may be a need for further conversation to understand what and why the person did what they did, especially if you've provided feedback before. Use the Ladder of Inference to explore assumptions and intentions. Assuming you are able to get to a mutual understanding, ask your direct report to restate the commitment of what needs to be done going forward. Be sure to reinforce and follow up.

Chapter 9: PARTICIPATE

1. How do your direct reports know how they are doing and what difference it makes? What do you do well to keep them on track?

2. How intentional and effective are you with regard to matching your management style to your direct reports' ability and desire in a given situation?

3. Where have you experienced management style misalignment – where the ability and desire of the employee (perhaps yourself) didn't seem to align with how the employee was being managed?

4. Do you have regular one-to-ones with your direct reports? With your manager? What are some best practices you've experienced? What other ideas do you have for making one-to-ones even more effective?

5. How often and in what ways do you ensure all members of your team know how each other is doing?

Exercises:

1. Create a tracking process – perhaps a traffic-light check-in – to identify progress on important projects and goals.

2. Select a current or future project for one of your direct reports. Determine where that person is with respect to their ability and desire to do the task. Are there any variables that might cause you to adjust your management style in this situation?

3. If you have regular one-to-ones with your direct reports or manager, take time to ask each other what's working well and what could be even more valuable. If you don't have regular one-to-ones, choose at least one direct report to get started. Jointly decide on an agenda that could include such things as progress on SMART goals and projects, work relationships, career direction, or life in general. At the end of the conversation, conduct a mutual debrief and plan for when to meet next.

Chapter 10: PARTICIPATE – Part 2

1. How does the ABC model resonate with you?

2. What are some antecedents to behavior in your organization/team?

3. What are some consequences (perceived as positive or negative) in your organization/team?

4. How have you experienced consequences (perceived as positive or negative) reinforcing or changing behavior?

5. Do you agree that the lack of feedback – or neutral consequences - can be perceived as negative consequences? Give an example to explain your response.

6. Give an example of how you made behavioral choices based on the certainty, immediacy, frequency, or strength of possible consequences?

7. Which do you think is more useful to a manager: focusing on the antecedents or focusing on the consequences? Explain.

Exercise:

Consider the normal behaviors and actions of your direct reports. Make a list of as many antecedents and consequences as you can that seem to be in place in your organization. Determine which antecedents or consequences to adjust to get better performance results.

Chapter 11: PARTICIPATE – Part 3

1. What teambuilding experiences have you had with your direct reports? What were the purpose, process, and payoff?

2. Describe a teambuilding exercise you've participated in that you felt was particularly valuable for you and why.

3. What behavior/personality assessments have you used? What have you learned about yourself through the process?

4. As you consider your Johari Window with respect to your team, what have you intentionally done to enlarge the size of your public domain/arena?

5. Assuming you've done something above, what have been any of your blind spots you became aware of? What have you done as a result of that awareness?

6. How much do your direct reports understand about your collective work processes? How might you increase that understanding?

7. "Work can be a spiritual experience ... one in which I feel connected to something greater than myself and through that connection I contribute something that matters – that makes a positive difference. Further that I may make that contribution in relationship with other people with whom I have mutual care and respect. And, that we periodically celebrate our efforts and remember together our connection to a purpose greater than ourselves." How do you respond to this comment? How have you considered your work as a spiritual experience?

Exercises:

1. Design and participate in a teambuilding process with your direct reports. There are numerous resources to pick from for various activities depending on your purpose.

2. If you haven't done a personality/behavior assessment recently, consider completing one. Check with HR to see what resources they have. There are plenty of assessment tools on the market and in the public domain.

3. Bring your team together to go over the Johari Window. Then facilitate a "Gift of Feedback" exchange following the process as described in the book. If you are uncomfortable facilitating this, ask HR or another manager for assistance.

4. With your direct reports, draw a process flow map of the work done by your team. Identify the critical handoffs and what is working or not working well at each transition point.

Chapter 12: EVALUATE

1. Does your organization have a defined process and/or forms for conducting performance evaluations? Describe how it works.

2. How is any rating system perceived in your organization? If and how do other managers and HR review the ratings you assign?

3. What's been your experience in this or other organizations with respect to having your performance formally evaluated? What worked well? What improvements can you suggest?

4. What are you doing to ensure your direct reports have no surprises come review time?

5. How do you use third party feedback and from whom?

6. In your process, what is reviewed and planned forward? You might include such things as SMART goals, performance results, how the person interacted with others, how the person demonstrated the organization values, professional development plan, and/or next period's goals.

7. In your experience, how close have your assessments been to what your direct reports expected? If they were dissimilar, what were some reasons for the discrepancies? How were they resolved?

8. In your organization, how closely related are performance evaluations and compensation adjustments? Why?

Exercises:

1. Look over your SMART goals and do a self-assessment. What do you want to celebrate? What adjustments do you need to make before your official review time?

2. Create or review your professional development plan. Are you on track with where you want to be? What else do you need to learn or do to be even better in your current role? What can you learn or do to prepare for another role you'd like to have?

3. Review your notes on your direct reports. How necessary, relevant and sufficient are they for helping you prepare for the next performance evaluation? Make any additional notes and plan how to keep up to date with what you'll want to refer back to.

4. Prepare for an upcoming performance evaluation of one of your direct reports. What will be the agenda? What data do you plan to share? How do you believe your comments will compare to that person's self-assessment? How will you determine a rating? How and when will you discuss any compensation adjustment?

Chapter 13: PARTICIPATE – Part 4

1. Describe a situation in which you – or a direct report – were caught in an activity trap. How did you recognize you were in it? How did you get out? How are you preventing getting caught again?

2. How do you distinguish between time management and priority management? What difference does it make?

3. If you create lists, especially with some indication of priority, how many high-priority tasks do you typically have on your list at any given time? How effective have you been in getting to all of them on time?

4. What tasks in your priority boxes 3 or 4 do you never seem to get to? What is the impact of that? If you need to take action on something that's been languishing in box 3 or 4, what do you need to do to put some or all of it in your High 5? What opportunities are there to delegate some of those tasks? (See Chapters 14-16.)

Exercises:

1. Create a priority matrix of your tasks for next week. Be sure to list no more than your High 5 in priority box 1. It may help to ask, "Who is this important to and why?" and "When does that person need it – not just when they want it, but really need it?" Also as you populate your matrix, remember that larger projects can be broken down into chunks for planning purposes.

2. Encourage your direct reports to create their own priority matrices for next week. Review with them to ensure that your priorities and expectations are in alignment with theirs.

3. Create additional priority matrices for yourself using different timeframes – one day, one month, one quarter, one year, three years. You may also want to do a similar process for your personal life – possibly with any significant other(s). What insights did you gain from this exercise?

CHAPTER 14: DELEGATE

Author's recommendation: Work through the three chapters of DELEGATE as a cluster.

1. As a manager, what have you typically delegated to others? To whom did you delegate what and why?
2. How has what you've delegated to whom and why changed through an employee's Training, Sustaining, and Gaining phases?
3. Have you ever hesitated to delegate a task to someone? What have been the reasons for your hesitation? If you could rewind the clock, what would you do differently?
4. What has been your most successful delegation to date? What were some of the reasons it went so well?

Exercises:

1. Create a spreadsheet as Ariel did. Label it "Delegation Possibilities". Column A is a list of "Possible Tasks". Start with a list of some of your generic tasks such as report writing, reviewing documents, attending meetings, talking with clients, and so on.
2. Add tasks that are in your Priority Matrix boxes 2, 3, and 4, especially if they've needed attention for some time.
3. Carefully eliminate any task that you believe CANNOT be delegated even if a right person could be identified and would have time. What you'll have left is a first draft of some tasks that you could possibly delegate.

Chapter 15: DELEGATE – Part 2

Note - this is a continuation from the preceding DELEGATE chapter.

1. In your experience, what kinds of tasks have been most valuable for you to delegate – those that are short-term and possibly urgent or those that are longer term? Explain.

2. As you consider what tasks to delegate, how do you determine what skills and knowledge will be necessary to accomplish the task?

3. To whom have you delegated parts or all of a task beyond your direct reports? Why? How did that work?

4. How do you know who has what skills and knowledge or could/should develop some specific skill or knowledge?

5. What are some of reasons you might select a particular person to whom to delegate a task?

Exercises:

1. Continue with the spreadsheet by adding a column B labeled "Organizational Priority". Next to each task in column A that you considered possible to delegate, indicate the relative organizational priority.

2. Create column C labeled "Special Skills and Knowledge" to indicate what will be needed to complete each task. You may want to create a separate coded index of skills and knowledge.

3. Create a Capacity Matrix. Along the side list all the skills and knowledge needed to do the work of your

team/department. (If you did Exercise 2 above, you already have the codes you created.) Across the top list all the people to whom you might delegate something. Start with your own direct reports. You can add others later. Once you have the Matrix in place, code each intersecting box with each person's current level of expertise – high, medium, or low – and the future level of expertise you'll need from that employee in say, 6 months or a year. So for any given skill/knowledge, you should be able to indicate at what level each employee is currently working and if/when the employee may need development to raise their expertise.

4. Brainstorm all the possible constituents to whom you could delegate some or all of a task. You may want to start with categories then go on to specific names. Categories might include your direct reports, other employees, your manager, other managers, customers, vendors, and consultants.

5. Create column D labeled "Who could do this?" For each task, list by name who might be able to do the task with respect to expertise.

6. Create column E labeled "Readiness". Use "N" to indicate the person has the requisite skills/knowledge now or "T" to indicate the person would need some training.

7. Create column F labeled "Why?" to indicate the reason(s) to delegate that task to that person. These might include such things as to build team capacity, closeness to the situation, has the skills and knowledge, potential partnership, and so on.

Chapter 16: DELEGATE – Part 3

Note - this is a continuation from the preceding DELEGATE chapters.

1. How have your delegation conversations changed through the employee's Training, Sustaining, and Gaining phases? In what ways did you determine the person's ability and desire to do the task?

2. How has your performance monitoring changed from one delegated task to another? What worked well? What might you change going forward?

3. What have been or could be indications that you might need to adjust your delegation conversation or monitoring process with any specific person or situation?

4. When work has been delegated to you, were you clear on what to do and by when? What discussions did you have about how to do the task? What discussions did you have on why the task was important? What discussions did you have about why you were selected to do the task? What discussions did you have about the resources and kinds of support available to you, including path-clearing? What discussions did you have about your responsibility and authority to make decisions?

5. Review the questions from above while considering a few delegations you've done with your direct reports. What insights are you gaining about delegation?

Exercise:

Use your "Delegation Possibilities" worksheet to select a task to delegate to a specific person. Prepare for and have a delegation conversation that includes:
   * clarifying the task that needs to be done
   * why it's important
   * the expected results and timeline
   * why you selected this person for this task
   * what resources will be needed
   * what support will be available
   * the level of decision-making authority
   * how you will monitor progress
   * explore any questions or concerns
   * be sure you are both in agreement and have the employee's commitment
   * end the discussion with support and encouragement

Chapter 17: ELEVATE

1. In your organization, how do you determine if and when to promote an employee?

2. When you've promoted someone, especially if to a position outside your team, what kind of hole has it left, if any? How did you handle that?

3. How does your organization – or do you – determine who are the high potential employees?

4. When you've had two or more internal candidates appropriate for promotion to a single position, how have you determined which one, if any, to promote?

5. Have you ever felt you were passed over for a promotion opportunity? What reactions did you experience? What did you do about it?

6. Have you ever had a direct report that was not selected for an internal promotion? What discussion did you have with that person to help him/her understand why the selection went a different way? What behavior changes, if any, did you notice as a result of being passed over?

7. Are you known as a manager who actively seeks growth opportunities for your employees or as one who wants to hold on to the best people? Explain any evidence for your answer. Is there anything you might want to change?

Exercise:

Create a matrix labeled "Potential to Elevate". Label the horizontal axis "Job Requirements" and label each column "Developmental", "Growing Competence", "Fully Competent", or "Mastery" to represent a person's knowledge and skills to do the current job. Label the vertical axis "Performance Rating" and have a row for each of your organization's performance rating levels, starting with the highest rating at the top. Write the name of each of your direct reports in the box that corresponds to where you see their current level of performance. What does this completed grid show you about who might be ready for a promotion?

Chapter 18: ELIMINATE, REMEDIATE and REINTEGRATE

1. Have you ever had an employee who was in Draining? Was the draining due to a lack of ability and/or a lack of desire? Explain your reasoning.

2. What actions did you take to try to get the employee back to performing at the Target Performance Level? What worked well? What might you do differently?

3. What were some barriers to performance that you've experienced in your own work? How did you address those barriers and try to eliminate them?

4. What are some of the most common barriers to performance that your employees experience? What have you done to try to eliminate them – or at least find workarounds?

5. If you determined that lower performance was due to insufficient ability, what did you do to address the problem? What worked well? What might you have done differently?

6. If you determined that lower performance was due to a decline in desire, what did you do to address the problem? What worked well? What might you have done differently?

7. How might lower performance due to burnout differ from lower performance caused by insufficient ability or decreased desire? How have you handled burnout in yourself or others?

8. If and how does motivation differ in the Training and Sustaining phases from motivation in the Draining phase?

Exercises:

1. Identify a current situation where you perceive an employee is in the Draining phase. Work your way through the Mager-Pipe Analyzing Performance Problems as described in the book. Remember, how you have the performance discussion will depend greatly on whether the gap is due to ability and/or desire. Consider what barriers might be making it difficult to achieve desired results. Consider if and what adjustments you may need to make in antecedents or consequences.

2. Have a performance-gap discussion with the employee from the exercise above. After setting context and purpose, determine if you and the employee are seeing the same gap. Then explore what the employee considers are possible reasons for the gap. The Mager-Pipe questions may be useful during the conversation. Once the reasons for the gap are relatively agreed on, explore ways for the employee to get back to the Target Performance Level. Remember, your intent is to work with the employee to get back on track, not to gather more evidence and justification for termination.

Chapter 19: MIGRATE

1. Does your organization have a philosophy or practice about moving someone who is draining in one position to a different position that might be a better fit? Explain any situations of which you are aware.

2. In your experience, has MIGRATE ever been used just to "pass the problem" on to someone else? Describe what worked or didn't work in that situation. What would you recommend to do differently, if anything?

3. Have you ever experienced an employee "jumping" to another position just to get ahead in their own career? What was the impact on the organization?

4. What recommendations do have for guidelines on "dumping" or "jumping"?

5. Have you ever loaned an employee to another part of your organization or outside your organization? What were the reasons for doing so? What was the impact on the organization? What was the impact on the individual?

6. Have you ever "adopted" an employee loaned from another part of the organization or from outside? What were the reasons for doing so? What was the nature of the work or special project with which that person was involved? What was the impact on the organization? What was the impact on the individual?

Exercises:

An employee does not need to be in the Draining phase for this to be a powerful exercise. Consider also those who are in Sustaining or Gaining phases and how this might be useful for their professional development, or at least some variety and new challenges for awhile.

1. Do some research on possibilities for temporary or permanent migration. Consider special internal assignments as well as external. Determine what timelines might be appropriate. Describe what positive benefits there might be for the organization and for an individual for any potential assignment.

2. Use the DELEGATE process to explore with an employee what opportunities might be appropriate and why. Also explore how to fill the hole that may be created by that employee being away temporarily or permanently.

3. If the MIGRATE assignment is temporary, stay in touch with the employee to discuss what is being learned and how those lessons will be useful when returning to the previous position.

Chapter 20: TERMINATE

1. Describe your organization's progressive discipline policy. How well does it seem to be working? Is the policy in alignment with your organization's values? Is it up-to-date with respect to government guidelines? What recommendations might you have to make it more effective?

2. In your experience, what has been the success of any performance improvement plan in your organization? What actions tend to lead to success? Where does the process fall short?

3. Have you ever had an employee leave voluntarily? Have you ever left a position of your own accord? What led to the decision to move on? What was the impact on the organization?

4. Have you ever terminated an employee or been terminated yourself? Describe the situation and process. What was done well in this difficult situation? Given the circumstances, what could have made it a better experience?

5. How did the employee respond when told he/she was being terminated? Describe any experiences you've dealt with where there was shock, denial, crying, or anger. How did you handle these? What might you have done differently?

6. What questions and concerns do you have about progressive disciplinary action including termination? Who can you talk with in your organization to get more clarity and understanding?

Exercise:

Many managers have never had to terminate an employee due to poor performance, an infraction against company policies and values, or organizational restructuring. If you might ever face that challenge, preparation and practice – along with help from your manager and HR – will help you be ready. For now, you may need to imagine a situation(s) to prepare a script, anticipate possible reactions from the employee, then practice through role-play. If you have a pending conversation at this time, do the same thing – but it's more likely to feel like real-play. Check your organization's policies and practices to determine if a third person and/or security should be present.

Chapter 21: RUMINATE

1. What have you learned or re-learned about management in the last few months? What else do you need to learn to be even better?

2. Of the 18 Tasks of Management – which three are your strongest skills? What do you need/want to focus on to be an even better manager?

3. What management tasks were missing from the book that you feel are critical to your job? How well do you perform those tasks? What else do you need to learn?

4. What is the difference between being a manager and being a leader? What are the implications of those differences for you and for your professional growth/career?

Exercises:

1. Share a few personal management stories using concepts and language from the book. Describe how someone went through the Phases of Employee Performance punctuated with various Management Tasks that you intentionally performed.

2. Flip through Ariel's Binder as a quick review. Use these materials and your own experience to help others become even better managers.

3. Review the list of best practices you've been compiling. What are two or three practices you do particularly well? What are two or three practices that you will focus on improving in the next few months? How will you (continue to) get feedback on how you are doing as a manager?

4. Share feedback on the book's Facebook page www.Facebook.com/WhatDoesItMeanToBeAManager or email the author at Gil@ManagingHorizons.com.

Made in the USA
Lexington, KY
10 April 2015